Acting Edition

HIGH SCHOOL BAKE-OFF

BY GINNA HOBEN

This work is published by Playscripts, an imprint of Concord Theatricals Corp.

No one shall make any changes in this title(s) for the purpose of production. No part of this book may be reproduced, stored in a retrieval system, scanned, uploaded, or transmitted in any form, by any means, now known or yet to be invented, including mechanical, electronic, digital, photocopying, recording, videotaping, or otherwise, without the prior written permission of the publisher. No one shall share this title(s), or any part of this title(s), through any social media or file hosting websites.

For all inquiries regarding motion picture, television, online/digital and other media rights, please contact Concord Theatricals Corp.

MUSIC AND THIRD-PARTY MATERIALS USE NOTE

Licensees are solely responsible for obtaining formal written permission from copyright owners to use copyrighted music and/or other copyrighted third-party materials (e.g. artworks, logos) in the performance of this play and are strongly cautioned to do so. If no such permission is obtained by the licensee, then the licensee must use only original music and materials that the licensee owns and controls. Licensees are solely responsible and liable for clearances of all third-party copyrighted materials, including without limitation music, and shall indemnify the copyright owners of the play(s) and their licensing agent, Concord Theatricals Corp., against any costs, expenses, losses and liabilities arising from the use of such copyrighted third-party materials by licensees. For music, please contact the appropriate music licensing authority in your territory for the rights to any incidental music.

IMPORTANT BILLING AND CREDIT REQUIREMENTS

If you have obtained performance rights to this title, please refer to your licensing agreement for important billing and credit requirements.

CHARACTERS
(AND THEIR BAKED GOODS)

OLIVIA – Highly driven. (Janice's Chocolate Chip Cookies.)

DUFFY – Here to help.

POSY – Selfless, earnest, a helper. (Sugar Cookies.)

JENNA – Future professional baker. (S'mosts Bars.)

MEG – Supports other people, has a creative streak. (Bumble Bread Loaf.)

REGGIE – Talented high achiever. (Vegan Maple Syrup Bars, Gluten-Free Oatmeal Chocolate Chip Cookies, Country Cream Cupcakes.)

MARCUS – Oddly competitive. (Brownie Bombs.)

BOB – Great intentions, doesn't bake.

COLLETTE – Passionate young activist. (Flaky Cakes.)

EVIE – Senior. She's so over high school she can barely keep her eyes open.

All characters are underclassmen (ages fourteen to seventeen), except for Evie who is seventeen or eighteen.

SETTING

High school auditorium. Early morning into first period.

NOTES ON PROPS

The baked goods can look realistic or not, but as a collection, they should look really impressive: colorful, large, stage-worthy. Have fun!

Text on the display cards should be big enough that at least some of the audience can make out the words.

It would be great if Bob's PowerPoint presentation could be projected on a big screen as a backdrop to the whole play.

ADDITIONAL NOTES

Dialogue that is italicized in brackets is not meant to be spoken. It's there so the actor knows where the thought is going.

No pauses unless indicated. The pace should be brisk!

PART ONE

(From the darkness.)

OLIVIA. Table!

POSY. Table!

OLIVIA. Display cards?

POSY. Display cards!

OLIVIA. Ten assorted batches of baked goods?

POSY. Baked goods en route!

OLIVIA. Lights?

(Beat.)

Lights?

POSY. I'm not on lights. Duffy?

DUFFY. *(Over a megaphone.)* Yo!

<table>
<tr><td>OLIVIA.</td><td>POSY.</td></tr>
<tr><td>Lights?</td><td>Lights?</td></tr>
</table>

(The lights come on to reveal **OLIVIA** *and* **POSY** *with platters heaping with cookies.)*

POSY. Oh, that's helpful! Light is helpful. Thanks, Duffy.

*(***DUFFY*** enters.)*

DUFFY. *(Still – needlessly – on the megaphone.)* You are welcome.

POSY. *(Amused.)* You sound like a robot.

DUFFY. *(His best robot impression.)* I. Am. Not. A. Robot.

*(***POSY*** *laughs.* ***OLIVIA*** *does not.)*

OLIVIA. Okay. Let's get to work! I'm seeing chocolate things over here and non-chocolate things over there.

POSY. Or we could mix them up so no one gets palate fatigue.

OLIVIA. Palate fatigue?

POSY. Oh, yeah. You know, like when you're eating something – even something you love – but then after too much of it, it's just not as good? Like with a really big order of frozen yogurt?

DUFFY. *(Back on the megaphone.)* That has never happened to me.

OLIVIA. Are you going to do that all morning?

*(***DUFFY*** *lowers the megaphone.)*

POSY. *(Back to palate fatigue.)* Like not even with pancakes?

DUFFY. No...

POSY. Spicy foods?

DUFFY. I don't think so...

POSY. Vegetables?

DUFFY. *(Thinks.)* No. Hmm-mm. Never run out of palate.

OLIVIA. He really loves food.

POSY. Yeah, sure, so do I, but sometimes, you can just stop tasting a food.

DUFFY. *(Considers this.)* I don't knoooow...no, I don't think I do.

POSY. You probably do. Everybody does.

DUFFY. Nope, not me. But if you want to run an experiment with loaded potato skins, I'm in.

OLIVIA. Okay, we'll alternate chocolate and non-chocolate platters as soon as the other entries get here. We can start making the display cards now.

*(Indicating **POSY**'s baked goods.)* Posy, what do you call those?

POSY. *(Despite her casual response, she is very proud of her entry.)* They don't have a specific name. Just sugar cookies.

> *(Unthinkingly, **OLIVIA** includes the word "just" on the display card. As **OLIVIA** writes...)*

DUFFY. What's in them?

POSY. Butter, sugar, flour, vanilla, the usual stuff.

DUFFY. Is there frosting?

POSY. No.

DUFFY. Sprinkles?

POSY. Hmm-mm.

DUFFY. Nuts? I'm allergic to some nuts.

POSY. No nuts.

OLIVIA. Do you think we need to list the ingredients of everything?

POSY. Oh, probably. For allergies.

DUFFY. *(Back to **POSY**'s cookies.)* What's special about them?

OLIVIA. Or we could just say you can't be a taste tester if you have allergies.

POSY. That's not very inclusive though.

POSY. *(To* **DUFFY**.*)* I guess, it's the attention required. You have to be really precise for them to come out right. But when they do – [*...they are wonderful.*]

OLIVIA. Inclusive. You're right. What do we do? Different categories? The nut allergies and the non-nut allergies?

POSY. But what about gluten-free diets? And vegans?

OLIVIA. I feel pretty confident that the "GFs" and vegans won't pay us money to eat baked goods.

POSY. Fair point. But now I'm wishing I made something that everyone can enjoy.

>   (**REGGIE** *enters with a catering cart overflowing with three types of goodies. This is going to be a real competition.)*

REGGIE. I did!

>   *(All heads turn.)*

OLIVIA. *(A little too formal.)* Hello, Reggie.

REGGIE. *(Matching her tone.)* Hello, Olivia.

OLIVIA. Welcome. What did you bake?

REGGIE. Cookies, cupcakes, and bars.

DUFFY. *(À la* The Wizard of Oz.*)* Oh my.

POSY. Oh! That could be a good way to display.

OLIVIA. What could?

POSY. Cookie entries here...cupcakes here...and bars over here.

OLIVIA. *(Earnestly; she needs this to work.)* And that won't cause palate fatigue?

POSY. Not if I do it right. Here, Reggie, why don't you give me the cookies first. Olivia is labeling everything –

OLIVIA. Wait, wait, wait. He can't have three entries.

REGGIE. Why not? They're all registered.

OLIVIA. That's…that triples your chance of winning.

REGGIE. Only if one of them is the best. Maybe they're all terrible.

DUFFY. Are they terrible?

REGGIE. No.

OLIVIA. I'm going to have to run this by Mrs. Parks.

REGGIE. Already did.

OLIVIA. And she said yes?

REGGIE. Well, once I explained Baking Inclusiveness…

POSY. Plus, we kind of need all three entries. Our tasters are paying for ten samples. And we have exactly ten entries registered.

OLIVIA. Right. Okay. So, what do you call those cookies?

REGGIE. Gluten-Free Oatmeal Chocolate Chip.

>*(As* **OLIVIA** *writes down the name and* **POSY** *places the cookies on the display table…)*

DUFFY. Oh, I love oatmeal chocolate chip! Can I try one?

REGGIE. Are you a taster?

DUFFY.	**OLIVIA.**
Yes.	No.

REGGIE. You are?

DUFFY.	**OLIVIA.**
No.	Yeah, okay.

REGGIE. This should be easier. Duffy, are you paying the tasting fee for the chance to vote?

DUFFY. Olivia said I can't.

OLIVIA. I just said "okay"!

DUFFY. No, that's alright.

REGGIE. Why is she in charge of what you do?

DUFFY.
She's not.

OLIVIA.
I'm not.

DUFFY. …It's just that since we're dating, Olivia felt that it wouldn't be fair of me to taste. She wants to win fair and square.

REGGIE. *(Indicating* **OLIVIA***'s cookies.)* With those?

OLIVIA. Yes. I mean, maybe.

> (**OLIVIA** *reveals the display card for her treat:* "*Janice's Chocolate Chip Cookies.*")

REGGIE. Janice's Chocolate Chip Cookies?

OLIVIA. Yes.

REGGIE.
Who's Janice?

POSY.
Who's Janice?

OLIVIA. Nobody knows. But this cookie recipe has been in my family for decades. Maybe centuries. They're a huge hit at sleepovers!

REGGIE. Yeah, she's not gonna win.

POSY. What else do you have, Reggie?

REGGIE. Vegan Maple Syrup Bars…

> (**OLIVIA** *writes a display card,* **POSY** *places the bars on the display table.)*

> *(Continuing.)* …and Country Cream-Filled Cupcakes.

> (**OLIVIA** *writes a new display card.)*

POSY. What's "country cream"?

REGGIE. Just the best cream filling…in the whole country! I created it.

POSY. Wow, that's amazing.

> (**POSY** *tries to take the cupcakes to add them to the display table.*)

REGGIE. *(Not yielding his cupcakes.)* It is amazing.

POSY. Want me to...? *[add them to the table.]*

REGGIE. I'll do it. They're fragile.

> (**REGGIE** *places the cupcakes and their display card where* **POSY** *indicates.* **MARCUS** *enters, dramatic, as always.*)

MARCUS. Hail, Reginald! Fellow Bake-ists.

REGGIE. Go away, Marcus. The contest hasn't started yet.

MARCUS. Still setting up, are we?

REGGIE. Yes. Now, go away.

MARCUS. I bite my thumb at you, Reginald! I'm here to compete. With my own entry!

OLIVIA. *(Unaware of any tension.)* Oh! I'm making display cards. What's your treat called?

REGGIE. Marcus, you don't care about baking. What are you doing?

MARCUS. I'm here to take you DOWN, Reginald Arthur Germain!

POSY. Well, there are several contestants, so technically – *[...you'd have to beat us all.]*

MARCUS. DOWN!

> *(To* **OLIVIA**.*)* Brownie Bombs. Bam!

OLIVIA. Did you say "bomb" as in "weapon"?

MARCUS. As in "an explosion in your mouth"!

> *(Mimics an extravagant explosion.)*

REGGIE. Ugh. Drama students.

POSY. Aren't you a drama student, Reggie? I thought I saw you in rehearsal for *Romeo and Juliet*.

MARCUS. We shall not speak of it!

REGGIE. To be clear: I've never taken the drama class here, but, yes, I was cast in –

MARCUS. SHHHHHH!

(Silence.)

REGGIE. ...the school play. Ever since then, Marcus has created this ridiculous rivalry between us.

*(***JENNA** *and* **MEG** *enter with platters of baked goods. Because of* **MARCUS** *and* **REGGIE**, *the girls go unnoticed.)*

It's not even a big role!

MARCUS. "There are no small parts, only small actors."

REGGIE. Whatever.

MARCUS. You don't even care! That's what kills me; you don't even care!

REGGIE. I care! I like plays and I like getting involved in things.

MARCUS. You think you care more about that role than I do?

REGGIE. Why does it matter? I got the part and I'm doing a good job. I'm having fun.

MARCUS. That's right. It's all just fun and games to you!

REGGIE. Oh, that's rich coming from the guy at the baking contest who's never shown an interest in baking.

MARCUS. Well played, opponent. Well played.

REGGIE. I'm not your opponent!

MARCUS. We're both in this contest, aren't we?

REGGIE. You can't be serious! The rest of us are actually interested in a baking club. Please go away.

MARCUS. Perhaps I will... Perhaps I will... What say you to a little challenge, Reginald? Suppose we each deliver the lines of the role you sequestered. The assembled shall choose the best delivery. If I win, I stay and compete in the baking contest. If you win, I will take my leave immediately.

POSY. I think "take my leave" means he'll go away and not enter the baking contest.

REGGIE. Deal!

MARCUS. You first.

> *(As the group shuffles around creating an open space and **REGGIE** steps into it:)*

JENNA. *(Quietly, to **MEG**.)* So, they're having a contest within a contest?

MEG. *(Quietly, to **JENNA**.)* I think it's a contest to enter the contest.

MARCUS. *(Re his supposed advantage.)* There is NO CONTEST!

*(To **REGGIE**.)* Begin, sir.

REGGIE. *(Confident, clear, sensible choices. He faces out, as if at an audition.)*
I do beseech you, sir, have patience.
Your looks are pale and wild, and do import
Some misadventure.

> *(The group politely applauds as **REGGIE** leaves the open space and **MARCUS** "takes stage.")*

MARCUS. *(Facing out, as if at an audition.)* Romeo and Juliet. Act Five, Scene One. The role of Balthasar.

REGGIE. *(Realizing he omitted this info.)* Uh, same.

MARCUS. *(A deep understanding of speaking and acting Shakespeare. Not overdone. Something truthful and genuine and connected. He's very, very good at this.)*

Her body sleeps in Capel's monument,
And her immortal part with angels lives.
I saw her laid low in her kindred's vault,
And presently took post to tell it you.
O, pardon me for bringing these ill news,
Since you did leave it for my office, sir.

> *(A beat of silence and then the group applauds enthusiastically.* **MARCUS** *takes a low bow.)*

REGGIE. Okay, so now what?

MARCUS. We could take a vote...or employ Ye Olde Applause-O-Meter.

REGGIE. For real?

OLIVIA. *(Noticing the newcomers. Happy for a change of subject.)* Jenna! Meg! You're here!

JENNA. You sound surprised...

OLIVIA. No, I just meant –

MARCUS. Silence!

MEG. *(Hushed. Re* **MARCUS.***)* Who is this guy?

DUFFY. *(Hushed.)* It's a play within a play. I mean, a contest within a contest. About a play.

MARCUS. Onlookers! What say you?

> *(No one knows how to respond.)*

People of Jonesville High, LET YOUR VOICES BE HEARD!

MEG. I don't know what this is all about, but that second guy was really good.

(General agreement that **MARCUS** *is a good actor.)*

REGGIE. Yeah, okay! You win, Marcus. You can stay. Just be cool, alright?

MARCUS. *(Evil villain victory laugh.)* AH-HAHAHAHAHA! AH-HAHAHAHAHA!

(As **MARCUS** *retreats:)*

REGGIE. So far from cool. So, so far.

OLIVIA. Okay. Moving on.

(To **JENNA** *and* **MEG.** *)* Welcome!

JENNA. Olivia, why are you, like, hosting? Like this is your event?

OLIVIA. Not just mine. It's for everyone.

JENNA. But only one president of the first-ever Jonesville High School Baking Club.

OLIVIA. Well, yeah, whoever wins...

JENNA. Yeah, but Olivia, you're already president of everything.

OLIVIA. Not everything...

JENNA. Just Student Council...

OLIVIA. "Vice" president. Evie is president...and really should be here by now.

DUFFY. And you're editor of the paper...

OLIVIA. That's different than "president"...

JENNA. And captain of the volleyball team, right?

MEG. And –

OLIVIA. Okay, okay. I like leadership roles.

JENNA. So do colleges.

OLIVIA. Sure. Yeah, I guess.

JENNA. But it's not like you're going to culinary school, are you?

OLIVIA. Oh, no. Is there even a degree in that?

JENNA. Yes. If a person wanted to go that route.

OLIVIA. Oh. Well, may the best baker prevail!

MARCUS. *(Louder than necessary.)* Huzzah!

OLIVIA. So, Jenna, what did you bring?

JENNA. Why do you want to know?

OLIVIA. So, I can write it on a display card. Like all of the others.

JENNA. I'll write it myself.

OLIVIA. I think the handwriting should be uniform, don't you?

JENNA. I don't think anyone gives a sugar cookie about uniform handwriting at a bake-off.

OLIVIA. They do.

JENNA. They don't.

OLIVIA. They do.

JENNA. They don't.

MEG. You can make me a display card. I made Bumble Bread.

POSY. Ooh, what's Bumble Bread?

MEG. Um, you know, like, um, flour, eggs, cinnamon...

DUFFY. I love all those things.

MEG. And zucchini.

REGGIE. Oh, I think my mom makes something like that.

MEG. With shredded cabbage...

DUFFY. *(Less enthusiastic.)* Oh.

MEG. And ham.

REGGIE. Ham? Did you say ham? Did she say ham?

MEG. Yeah. Yep. Ham.

POSY. Oh, so it's a savory thing?

MEG. Mm-hmm. Except for the chocolate-covered olives.

　　(Beat.)

POSY. And where does it get its name?

REGGIE. From somebody bumblin' round the kitchen?

MEG. Oh, I don't know. That's just what came to mind.

REGGIE. Meg, you can't win a baking contest with a food that pairs chocolate and ham.

DUFFY. *(Not altogether turned off by this chocolate-ham notion.)* I don't know...

REGGIE. I know. It's a really weird choice.

MEG. Yeah, I guess.

JENNA. She's a really good friend.

OLIVIA. What's that supposed to mean?

JENNA. Meg knew we needed one more entry to reach ten. But she wouldn't sabotage me. She wants me to win because she supports my interest in culinary school.

OLIVIA. So she's throwing the competition?

　　(To **MEG**.*)* You're throwing it?

MEG. I haven't thrown anything. What?

POSY. "Throwing" is intentionally giving up. Because you don't care. Athletes do it sometimes. "Throw" a game.

MARCUS. Or an actor can "throw" a performance.

POSY. ...Because they're proving a point.

MARCUS. *(Pointed.)* Or they don't care.

MEG. Oh, no, no. I care.

OLIVIA. About Bumble Bread?

MEG. Yeah. Yes! It's good.

REGGIE. That can't be true.

    *(**MEG** shrugs.)*

OLIVIA. Jenna, can you give me the name of your treat again, please?

JENNA. No, because I didn't give it to you a first time.

POSY. You know Jenna, she really does have great handwriting.

MEG. Yeah, she does.

REGGIE. You really do. It's like a font.

    *(Standoff between **OLIVIA** and **JENNA**.)*

OLIVIA. So, what are they called, Jenna?

JENNA. *(Intentionally creating a name too long for the display cards.)* Vanilla Sugar-Coated, Toasted –

OLIVIA. *(Writing carefully.)* Slow down, slow down...

JENNA. ...Marshmallow Blondie Bars with a Hazelnut Ribbon Glaze.

OLIVIA. That's not gonna / fit.

JENNA. And Chocolate Sprinkles.

OLIVIA. *(Understanding **JENNA**'s ploy.)* Seriously?

JENNA. À la Mode.

REGGIE. You brought ice cream?

JENNA. No. Darn it. You can cross off that last part.

OLIVIA. How about Marshmallow Bars?

JENNA. *(Not giving in so easily.)* Mmm…

REGGIE. Or Hazelnut Blondies?

JENNA. No, no, it has to say "marshmallow."

MEG. How about Sugar Bombs?!

MARCUS. Already taken. Brownie Bombs right here.

(*Another mimicked explosion.*)

POSY. S'mores? They're kinda like s'mores.

JENNA. That's close… But they're not just s'mores… They're s'most!

(*General cheering from all except* **OLIVIA**, *who roughly scribbles out the word "S'mosts" on a display card. It is far from the pretty handwriting we have seen so far.* **POSY** *adds Jenna's treat and display card to the display table. Meanwhile, mostly unnoticed,* **BOB** *enters. He wears a suit and carries a rather grown-up laptop case.*)

BOB. Hi. Is this where we set up for the competition?

OLIVIA. Yes.

(*He opens a laptop.*)

You can tell me what your creation is called and Posy over here will add it to the lineup.

BOB. Oh. My title?

OLIVIA. Yeah, the name of it?

BOB. "The Decline of Home-Baked Grain-Based Foods and the Impact of Processed Snacks on Young People Today."

JENNA. I don't think that's going to fit on his display card.

OLIVIA. I'm sorry…that's the name of your / treat?

BOB. PowerPoint?

OLIVIA.	**BOB.**
What?	What?

BOB. Baking Club, right?

> *(Click!* **BOB** *displays the title slide of his PowerPoint presentation. Just then,* **EVIE** *enters, disheveled. Is she wearing pajamas? Debatable.)*

EVIE. Am I late?

> *(Except for* **OLIVIA***, the group responds "No," "We're still setting up," etc.)*

OLIVIA. A little, yeah.

EVIE. Okay.

OLIVIA. I mean, not if you're a contestant, but if you're supposed to be organizing and monitoring for voter fraud, then, yes, you're late.

EVIE. *(Ignoring* **OLIVIA***'s edge.)* 'S anybody have a pillow? I'm exhausted.

> *(She drags a chair up to the treats table and tries to go to sleep.)*

MEG. Who's that?

REGGIE. You don't know Evie Riley?

MEG. That's Evie? The Student Council President?

OLIVIA. Yeah. And she's supposed to be running this thing.

REGGIE. That doesn't seem likely.

DUFFY. She is so seriously lackadaisical.

MEG. Dang. Nice vocabulary, Duff.

*(General agreement that **EVIE** is unmotivated and that **DUFFY** used an A-list word.)*

OLIVIA. I've never seen anything like it. She used to be so motivated, but she doesn't do anything anymore. It's kind of a miracle she's here.

JENNA. Why'd she volunteer?

EVIE. *(Without lifting her head.)* I heard there'd be snacks.

OLIVIA. We proposed the idea back in the fall. She seemed really excited about it, but now I think she was just trying to prove herself to be a strong leader so colleges would favor her applications.

JENNA. Like you?

OLIVIA. *(Ouch.)* It's true that I want to get into a good program at a good college. And, yes, I guess I feel like I have to prove myself.

JENNA. *(Real empathy.)* Tell me about it.

(A moment to connect. Maybe they're not so different.)

OLIVIA. But now that Evie got into her second choice, she's done. She does only the absolute minimum required. It's so sad.

MEG. Senioritis. It happens to even the best students…

MARCUS. *(Out of nowhere, again managing to startle everyone.)* DUHN-DUHN-DUHN!

*(As a group, they gasp or shriek, realize it was **MARCUS**, and move on.)*

JENNA. Okay. So, now what?

OLIVIA. Are you genuinely asking me what we should do?

JENNA. *(Without snark this time.)* I'm pretty sure it's the vice president's duty to step up if the president is napping.

(General agreement from the group.)

OLIVIA. Well, as soon as the bell rings for homeroom, all the contestants should clear the space. Anyone who signed up to taste will come down, pay the fee to Duffy, and try everything here on display. Then they write down their vote on their ballot and drop it in the ballot box. Evie – assuming she wakes up – will count the votes and announce the results. Any food left over is on sale at lunchtime. All the proceeds go toward new supplies and ingredients for Baking Club.

MARCUS. And the baker with the most votes becomes CHAMPION!

POSY. Um, "President."

JENNA. Of the first-ever Jonesville High School Baking Club.

MARCUS. Great. Whatever.

JENNA. Do you even know what baking is?

MARCUS. Uh...yeah, it's baking stuff.

(Click! **BOB** *pulls up a slide with bullet points of his definition of baking.)*

BOB. It's the combining of raw ingredients – typically grain-based – then placing them in a heightened consistent heat for a designated duration resulting in one or more chemical changes that create something edible.

(Click! Next slide: a happy consumer of baked goods. Maybe **BOB** *himself.)*

And delicious.

JENNA. *(Back to* **MARCUS**.*)* ...which is really important to those of us who will pursue this as a career.

REGGIE. And those of us with natural skill and talent.

DUFFY. And those of us with healthy appetites!

MARCUS. *(Voice escalating.)* And those of us –!

EVIE. *(Lifts head.)* Could you guys discuss this more… quietly?

> *(Head down.)*

POSY. So, um, we're mostly set up over here. I think I've managed to alternate the chocolate and the non-chocolate things –

JENNA. Wait. Why are mine first? I don't want to be first.

POSY. Just because of when you got here and because yours is a chocolatey entry.

JENNA. But you two are last, next to Bumble Bread. I want to be next to Bumble Bread.

OLIVIA. It's fine as it is.

JENNA. Well, can I trade with Brownie Bombs? See how his platter is on the inside of the display? I'd rather be on the inside of the display than the outside perimeter.

POSY. *(Resisting any change to her hard work and effective display.)* Um…

MARCUS. Fine with me. Outer or inner, a winner's a winner.

> *(**POSY** trades Jenna's S'mosts with Marcus's Brownie Bombs.)*

MEG. Hey, guys, there's this big empty spot in the middle.

POSY. Yeah. Yes. That's intentional.

OLIVIA. There's one more registered entry.

> *(**COLLETTE** enters with as much fanfare as possible. She definitely has a picket sign. Maybe she wears a helmet and roller-skates in. She's ready for action.)*

COLLETTE. FIGHT FOR FEMINISM! MADE FROM SCRATCH SETS US BACK! MADE FROM SCRATCH SETS US BACK!

> *(Baking Contestants react to* **COLLETTE**'s *preposterous statement. General chaos.)*

JENNA. Whoa, whoa, whoa. What are you saying?

COLLETTE. This Baking Club is a threat to feminism! The last thing teenage girls need is to be shoved back into the kitchen, barefoot / and sweaty...

MEG. Who said anything about feet?

REGGIE. Who said anything about girls?

COLLETTE. ...and relying on a spouse for every penny instead of forging her own career!

JENNA. Baking is a career.

OLIVIA. And I'm a feminist.

POSY. Me too.

MEG. Me too.

REGGIE. So am I.

MARCUS. I'm a bigger feminist than he is!

DUFFY. I'm a feminist.

> *(They all look to* **BOB**.*)*

BOB. Oh, yeah, totally. I, uh,

> *(Scrolling through his PowerPoint.)* I have a slide for that...

> > *(Click! Bob's slide reads, "A feminist is anyone who supports the rights of women.")*

> > *(Beat.)*

COLLETTE. Frauds! Posers! You're not feminists! How can you be feminists if you're dedicating all your time to serving others? I'm for Resistance! Independence! And Convenience!

(Bam! She throws down a load of prepackaged, processed, factory-made cupcakes.)

REGGIE. OMG. What are those?

OLIVIA. Wait, I don't think you can enter the contest if you're against the concept of baking from scratch.

*(Click! **BOB** presents a slide titled "The Decline of Home-Baked Grain-Based Foods.")*

REGGIE. Ahem! What are those things?

COLLETTE. I can enter. I spoke with Mrs. Parks. If I win, I do what I want with my presidency.

OLIVIA. But –

REGGIE. WHAT ARE THESE?

MEG. Oh, those are Flaky Cakes! My parents used to put them in my lunch.

JENNA. FLAKY CAKES?! Those are...! Those are...! They're...

MARCUS. *(Supplying the dramatic soundtrack.)* Duh Duh Duhn...!

ALL BUT COLLETTE & EVIE. STORE-BOUGHT!

*(Simultaneously... Click! **BOB** presents a slide titled "The Impact of Processed Snacks on Young People Today" that illustrates the concept in a boldly colored bar chart.)*

*(**EVIE** wakes with a start: "Whuh?" and knocks Marcus's brownies to the floor, rendering them inedible.)*

(General gasps and reactions.)

POSY. You knocked over Marcus's Brownie Bombs!

MARCUS. *(As in a Greek tragedy.)* NOOOOOO! SHAME strike your household! PESTILENCE AND SHAME! My dad worked all night to make those.

(Beat.)

REGGIE. Waywaywaywaywaywaywait. Your dad made those brownies? You can't compete with someone else's creation!

MEG. What about "Store-Bought" over here?

OLIVIA. No, that's not okay either. Right, Evie? Evie?

EVIE. *(Deep sigh. They're going to make her work.)* Well, we need a variety of entries, right? Otherwise, what are the tasters getting for their money? So, I think...as long as she's honest about it, she can enter the Flaky Cakes.

(General groans from the other competitors.)

REGGIE. Nope! Nope! No way. Marcus didn't make his entry: disqualified. Collette didn't make hers: disqualified.

OLIVIA. And yet, you made three entries and somehow that's fair?

REGGIE. Uh, do the math, Olivia. Without me, you don't really have much of a competition, do you? I bring the quality and the quantity.

MEG. Chill out, people. Don't you think the voters will recognize the quality of your home-baked goods over the Flaky-Dakies?

REGGIE. I do not.

JENNA. I'm actually okay competing with those crap-cakes.

OLIVIA. Those crap-cakes make billions of dollars a year.

JENNA. I know. That's how much confidence I have in S'mosts.

REGGIE. It's a baking competition!

COLLETTE. Hold on, hold on. It's actually a pretty interesting social experiment. Aren't you all kind of curious to see how the Flakies would rank?

ALL BUT COLLETTE. No/Not really.

COLLETTE. Couldn't it shine a light on what we've become as a society? Where our values lie? What matters?

DUFFY. Maayyybeee...?

OLIVIA. Duffy!

DUFFY. I mean, I'm not gonna vote for them, but –

OLIVIA. You're not voting at all...

DUFFY. Right, but if that's what the people want...?

OLIVIA & REGGIE. It's not what the people want!

COLLETTE. Oh, this is getting good...

EVIE. Uh, yeah, look, I have minimal interest in this contest, but I'm'onna hafta stand firm on the fact that none of us know what the people want. So.

(Finds something to use as a gavel, raps it.)

The Flakies stay. Reggie's three entries stay... But Marcus, you lied.

MARCUS. I didn't lie, I just didn't tell the truth.

POSY. Also, I don't think we can ask our voters to eat something that was on the auditorium floor.

*(**DUFFY** makes an audible but nonverbal "I don't know" as if he'd consider eating those brownies.)*

OLIVIA. But –! That leaves only nine! And I don't think – I mean, Bob's entry isn't even edible! No offense.

(Click! **BOB** *displays a slide that says "This presentation is not to be consumed.")*

BOB. None taken.

EVIE. Olivia, calm down. Ugh, you are such a…a…an underclassman. Eight baked goods is enough for a single teenager.

*(***DUFFY*** makes an audible but nonverbal "I don't know," suggesting eight baked goods is not enough for him.)*

Now, Marcus, I'm sorry I knocked over your brownies, but you cannot compete.

MARCUS. *(Bummed. Then, to* **REGGIE**.*)* You haven't seen the last of me, nemesis!

*(***MARCUS*** exits in all his dramatic glory.)*

MEG. Maybe he should've gotten your role in the play. He's not short on the drama. No offense.

REGGIE. Oh, none taken. You're not wrong.

EVIE. Hey. I heard what you guys said about me. I'm exhausted but I can't get any quality sleep so everything around me sort of seeps into my thoughts. Including my, oh what was it…? "Lackadaisical" nature?

(General discomfort.)

OLIVIA. We didn't mean to hurt your feelings, but –

EVIE. Whatever. You're a junior; you don't understand.

JENNA. Okay, then explain it to us.

EVIE. No, it's dumb.

MEG. What is? High school? Everybody knows that.

(General chuckles and agreement.)

EVIE. Yeah, exactly. Everyone in high school hates high school. All of us are rolling our eyes and making jokes and counting the days until we're out of here. Sure. And at the same time...what if the joke's on us? You know? Because in no time – and in my case, even less time – we're not only out of here, but we're not coming back. We're not coming back to this school or any school that communicates with our parents when we mess up. It's all on us now. Tuition, grades, whether we pass or fail. No one is checking if your homework is done. No one knows if you attend class or skip. And as annoying as high school is with teachers and coaches breathing down your back, and cliques, and "cool kids," and going to the prom or not going to the prom and all that... it is this known entity. You arrive at this building and go to your little locker and you have this list of classes you are going to take. Check! Check! Check! The rest of the day is yours to fill with your sports, or your play practice, or your cute little baking club. Check! Check! Check! But after this...after high school, those check marks are a lot harder to come by. No one hands you a list. What classes are you going to enroll in? What are you choosing as a major? WHAT ARE YOU DOING WITH YOUR LIFE?

(Beat.)

DUFFY. Okaaaaay...

OLIVIA. Okay.

POSY. Okay.

> *(**POSY** starts cleaning up the fallen brownies. **EVIE** helps.)*

EVIE. Yeah, okay.

JENNA. Okay?

MEG. *(To* **JENNA**, *reassuring about the contest – or maybe the future.)* It's gonna be okay.

COLLETTE. *(Shrugs.)* Okay, then.

    (Click! **BOB** *displays a slide that says "Okay.")*

REGGIE. This is not okay.

    (The bell rings.)

DUFFY. *(On the megaphone.)* Contestants! Clear the space!

    (Blackout!)

    (Upbeat music.)*

    (Not imperative, but recommended slideshow. A slide displays the image and title of each baked-good entry. They should all look really good: VEGAN MAPLE SYRUP BARS, JANICE'S CHOCOLATE CHIP COOKIES, FLAKY CAKES, BUMBLE BREAD, JUST SUGAR COOKIES, S'MOSTS, GLUTEN-FREE OATMEAL CHOCOLATE CHIP COOKIES, COUNTRY CREAM CUPCAKES.)

    (See Appendix for optional "Tasters Scene," a wordless movement piece to be performed in place of or in conjunction with the suggested slideshow.)

---

* A license to produce HIGH SCHOOL BAKE-OFF does not include a performance license for any third-party or copyrighted recordings. Licensees should create their own.

PART TWO

(Lights rise. Tasting and voting are over. **EVIE** *is asleep.* **DUFFY** *is counting votes and snacking.)*

DUFFY. Oh my gosh! This is unbelievable! I did not see this coming. Another one for S'mosts! Dude! This is neck and neck! ...and neck! Did you see this coming?

(No response. **DUFFY** *looks to* **EVIE**.*)*

Evie?

(Pause.)

Evie!

*(**EVIE** wakes with a start, maybe one of the baked goods is stuck to her cheek.)*

EVIE. Whaa–?

DUFFY. Evie, this is really close. I think you better double-check my results.

EVIE. I don't know if I can; I'm so seriously lackadaisical!

DUFFY. Ugh! I'm sorry I said that, okay? But, can you just...help?

EVIE. Yeah, okay. What?

DUFFY. Okay, I'll name the treat, you recount their votes.

EVIE. Right.

DUFFY. Vegan Maple Syrup Bars.

EVIE. Two votes.

DUFFY. Two vegans voted, so...okay. Next: Gluten-free Oatmeal Chocolate Chip Cookies.

EVIE. *(Impressed.)* Six votes!

DUFFY. Bob's Baking PowerPoint Presentation.

EVIE. *(Looks around.)* Um...

DUFFY. Yeah. No votes. Collette's processed, packaged, factory-made Flaky Cakes.

EVIE. *(Incredulous.)* Eleven votes? C'mon! These things are so processed they could survive for a century.

>   *(Getting drawn into the drama.)*

Next!

DUFFY. Olivia's Janice's Chocolate Chip Cookies.

EVIE. Twenty-nine votes. Who's Janice?

DUFFY. Nobody knows. Okay...

>   *(Creating suspense.)*

Bumble Bread.

EVIE. THIRTY VOTES?

DUFFY. I know! But, Evie, it's so good!

>   *(**DUFFY** holds out some Bumble Bread for **EVIE** to try.)*

EVIE. It's not.

DUFFY. It is!

EVIE. No way.

DUFFY. It is!

>   *(**EVIE** reluctantly eats the Bumble Bread.)*

EVIE. Oh. Oh! Oh my gosh. That's...that's really good! Is that...green olive?

DUFFY. Yes! Isn't it genius?

EVIE. Yeah, that's kind of genius. But what's that other flavor?

DUFFY. I DON'T KNOW! I've been racking my brains.

EVIE. Wow, so that beats Olivia's twenty-nine.

DUFFY. And there's more! Ready? Country Cream Cupcakes.

EVIE. *(Counting the votes.)* Country Cream Cupcakes... Also thirty votes! This is insane!

DUFFY. And there's more! What's more...than s'more?

EVIE.	**DUFFY.**
S'mosts!	S'mosts!

>　　(**EVIE** *scrambles to gather and double-check the S'mosts votes.)*

EVIE. *(Re the results.)* Oh. Oh, I see. Oh, wow. And you already counted these once?

DUFFY. I definitely did. And then twice. And then I woke you up.

EVIE. So many victories. I didn't think it would be so neck and neck.

DUFFY. ...and neck. Evie...there's more!

>　　(**EVIE** *scans the table and the surrounding area.)*

EVIE. No, I think I have them all.

DUFFY. Not possible. There are nine entries, including Bob's. How many have you counted?

EVIE. Eight, including Bob's. So what is it? Which one is missing?

DUFFY. I can't remember! How is this possible? I know I counted the votes of nine entries. I even tried them all.

EVIE. You ate the entries?

DUFFY. I didn't finish them. I just, you know, felt I should have a frame of reference for that which I was counting.

EVIE. Well, what does your clipboard say?

(**DUFFY** *checks.*)

DUFFY. *(Deflates.)* "Last one."

EVIE. What?

DUFFY. It was the last one that I was counting,

(*Starting to panic.*)

...but the display card was missing!

EVIE. Okay, okay, don't panic –

DUFFY. I'm panicking!

EVIE. Stay cool, Duffy, stay cool. Just, think back... What was the last thing you ate?

(**DUFFY** *closes his eyes.* **EVIE** *walks him back through his actions like hypnosis.*)

DUFFY. Something really delicious...

EVIE. Was it a cookie?

DUFFY. It was not a cookie.

EVIE. Was it a cake?

DUFFY. Not cake exactly...

EVIE. Was it cakey?

DUFFY. A little cakey, yes.

EVIE. Did it have chocolate?

DUFFY. It had "ahhhh..."

EVIE. Ahhh??? Almonds?

DUFFY. No...I'm allergic to almonds. "Aaaah..."

EVIE. Ahhh... Alternative ingredients like vegan or gluten-free?

DUFFY. Aaaahhh... Aaaahhhlll... AHL... OL... Olives!

(He opens his eyes.)

Bumble Bread!

EVIE. We already counted Bumble Bread!

DUFFY. I know but you asked me what was the last thing I ate and that was my favorite thing so I had seconds.

EVIE. Duffy!

DUFFY. Yes?

EVIE. You had one job!

DUFFY. I know, I just – Wait. Evie, you had one job! Counting the votes was your job. You asked me to help because you felt tired and then you went to sleep.

EVIE. Oh, so now it's my fault that you ate some of everything and then lost an entire stack of votes?

DUFFY. Yeah, dude, it kind of is.

EVIE. Shoot. It is my fault. I don't know what's happened to me. I used to be very responsible. And alert.

DUFFY. It's okay, Evie.

EVIE. ...And if I'm going to slack off, I usually choose someone just as responsible to take over.

DUFFY. Hey!

EVIE. No offense.

DUFFY. None taken. I guess I slacked off too. AARGH! We gotta find those votes!

> *(A fast-paced search ensues. Maybe music underscores.* * *Perhaps the stack of votes is discovered where* **EVIE** *was sleeping; basically, they were under her sleeping head.)*

DUFFY. FOUND THEM!

EVIE. YES! Okay. Which treat was it?

DUFFY. POSY'S JUST SUGAR COOKIES!

EVIE. YES! JUST SUGAR COOKIES!

DUFFY. Except, I don't think the "just" was intentional.

EVIE. Right! Of course. Okay, SO TELL ME!

DUFFY. I don't trust my numbers! What if they're wrong?

EVIE. Just TELL ME, Duffy!

DUFFY. Please count them! They have to be double-checked anyway.

> *(**EVIE** grabs the stack of votes and begins counting, some silent, some out loud. A pause. She takes and checks **DUFFY***'s clipboard.)*

EVIE. *(Regarding the number of Sugar Cookie votes that* **DUFFY** *recorded.)* Yep, that's what I got to. I guess we have a winner.

DUFFY. I guess we have a winner!

EVIE. Okay, well, go on and get everybody so we can announce the results.

DUFFY. I can't.

EVIE. Why not?

DUFFY. Some of them scare me.

---

*A license to produce HIGH SCHOOL BAKE-OFF does not include a performance license for any third-party or copyrighted recordings. Licensees should create their own.

EVIE. Oh. Yeah. They are a little scary. Here. Take this.

> *(She hands him a hunk of Bumble Bread.)*

For courage.

DUFFY. *(Munches. As he exits...)* How is this so GOOD?

EVIE. *(Alone. A discovery.)* That was fun. I'm exhausted.

> *(**EVIE** puts her head down and goes promptly to sleep on the clipboard. General murmurs and excitement as the contestants enter behind **DUFFY**. They form an oddly formal line. **MARCUS** is back.)*

DUFFY. Alright. Everyone's here. In an oddly formal line...

> *(They look at each other; each makes a deliberate attempt to appear casual.)*

...Evie! The results?

> *(**EVIE** emits a loud snore.)*

REGGIE. You've got to be kidding me!

> *(General groans.)*

OLIVIA. Go ahead, Duffy. You tell us.

DUFFY. No way! That's not my job. Can't someone just nudge her a little?

> *(Awkward beat.)*

POSY. I'll do it.

> *(Gently, to **EVIE**.)* Hey, Evie? It's time to announce the results. You know, of the baking contest? Evie?

> *(Nudge, nudge. Then, unexpectedly loud.)*

Evie!

EVIE. AAH! Oh my gosh, I thought you were that weird drama kid.

(*Awkward.* **MARCUS** *doesn't register it.*)

MARCUS. Which one of you is in drama?

POSY. Evie, it's time to announce the winner of the contest.

EVIE. (*Groggy, she glances at the clipboard.*) The sugar-bumble thing won.

(**EVIE** *pushes the clipboard across the table and goes back to sleep.*)

JENNA. What? What did she say?

MEG.	**POSY**.
Bumble?	Sugar?

(**JENNA** *and* **OLIVIA** *rush the clipboard. Everyone else backs away.*)

OLIVIA. I only got twenty-nine votes.

(**OLIVIA** *rushes off.* **JENNA** *is left with the clipboard and results.*)

MEG. What did she mean? Bumble? Or Sugar?

JENNA. You didn't win, Meg. But you got more votes than Olivia. You tied with Reggie's Country Cream Cupcakes.

MEG. (*Ecstatic.*) I did? Really I did?

REGGIE. (*Less than enthusiastic.*) Yay, us.

MARCUS. Oh, how the mighty have fallen! AH-HAHAHAHAHA!

REGGIE. Okay, Marcus, you can go to class now. You cheated, you proved your point, and now you got to see me fail.

MARCUS. Aaaaaaaaaaand: Scene!

REGGIE. Yeah, "scene." ...But what you don't realize is that it's not always about getting the part or winning the game or getting the most votes. I prepared, I did my best, and I got to be part of something.

*(As **MARCUS** digests this notion...)*

JENNA. Yeah, that's right; it's not always about getting the most votes, but this time I'm curious. Meg, how in the world do you beat out Reggie's fluffy, angelic, clouds-of-vanilla cupcakes with chocolate-covered olives? Chocolate-covered olives, Meg! We discussed this. We planned. We masterminded!

MEG. Yeah, right? We did, didn't we? But, ya know, once I got going, I don't know, it felt like, really exhilarating. To create something.

POSY. I know what you mean.

MEG. ...And I was starting to think I could make something good. You know? In the world.

REGGIE. Totally.

BOB. Yeah.

MEG. ...and also, chocolate-covered olives is a really time-consuming step, so I switched the milk chocolate coating with just a trace of pulverized unsweetened chocolate. And it turns out to really complement the cabbage. Who would've thought it, right? I mean, cabbage doesn't belong at this party, amiright?

(Expanding on the metaphor, but making it up as she goes.)

Unless it was invited by pulverized unsweetened chocolate. See? Imagine they show up together at like, prom, and everyone is like, "Cabbage? What is Cabbage doing here with Chocolate?" And Chocolate is like, "Guys, guys, guys, I've been coming to this party every year, and every year I'm basically crowned royalty, I mean, I'm Chocolate! But if the same ingredients are the only ones who come to the party over and over, can we ever grow? Can we ever expand?"

COLLETTE. I was with her until "prom."

REGGIE. It's just a metaphor.

MEG. The point is there are endless, unpredictable, positive outcomes, but we can't get to them unless we branch out a little.

POSY. So, Bumble Bread was just an experiment?

MEG. Yeah, but it definitely failed. A couple of times. Until finally I just covered the whole thing with shredded aged asiago. Because what isn't better with melted cheese?

DUFFY. Aged asiago!

MEG. *(Re how long the asiago was aged.)* Stravecchio.

(General reactions of awe.)

JENNA. Meg... I want to be mad at you...but that's... really...beautiful. What you said. Like, you get it. That's what it's all about. You get to be creative and original and experimental...and take all these separate things that are okay on their own, but when you put them together, they're fantastic.

> *(Click!* **BOB** *presents a slide that illustrates DRY INGREDIENTS + WET INGREDIENTS + HEAT = CAKE.)*

MARCUS. Wow. I'm sorry, I don't mean to make this about me –

(General groans from all.)

Touché, touché, mes amis. But, Jenna, what you just said...that's how I feel. That's all I want to do. I want to be creative and original and experimental...and I want to share that work. The way your cakes and cookies are a gift to those who consume them, a play is a gift to an audience!

REGGIE. Yeah, but...

MARCUS. In the theatre, we say "yes, and..."

REGGIE. Right. "Yes, and" ...it's not only about the audience or the person who gets to eat the cupcake. It's also about working together. I mean, it feels nice to win, but really I'm here to join the group. To be a part of something. To hear how Jenna combines flavors, or how Posy makes the perfect Sugar Cookie. Or how, like today, our combined efforts are going to start a brand-new club and raise the funds for the supplies. We're making something out of nothing!

MARCUS. I do that too...!

REGGIE. Yep, and you do it really well. You're a good actor, Marcus. But – I mean, *and* – you could do even more working with a group instead of competing against it.

MARCUS. I hear you. That, um, means a lot that you think I'm a good actor.

(*Beat.*)

Whoa, this bake-off is not what I expected. Mind blown!

(**REGGIE** *mimics an explosion, Marcus-style.* **MARCUS** *takes the joke.*)

I'm sorry I didn't take it seriously. You guys really created something!

JENNA. Something that literally nourishes others.

(*Beat.*)

COLLETTE. Oh. My. Chromosomes! I am such a jerk. I thought you were all reverting to some old-fashioned female stereotype. I didn't understand at all!

(Click! **BOB** *presents a slide from his presentation that says, "Baking: no longer stereotypically feminine or old-fashioned.")*

JENNA. And yet you still got eleven votes.

COLLETTE. NOOOOOO! Okay. New protest:

(She seizes the megaphone.)

End processed foods!

(Everybody cheers. As the cheers fade, **BOB** *raises his hand. No one knows how to respond to a raised hand.)*

REGGIE. You can just talk, Bob. There's no one in charge here – [*...to call on you.]*

BOB. Okay.

(To **JENNA**, *who still holds the clipboard with the results.)* I didn't get any votes, did I?

JENNA. Um, no. You didn't.

BOB. *(Nods.)* Yeah, I think I...I misunderstood the assignment.

POSY. Oh, this wasn't mandatory. Did you think you had to be here?

BOB. Oh, no, no. I wanted to be here.

(To all of them.) I have a deep appreciation for the culinary arts.

(Click! **BOB** *presents a slide defining "Culinary Arts.")*

Baking from scratch.

(Click! **BOB** *presents a slide defining "Baking from Scratch.")*

All cooking, in fact. I'm not the type to make any of those things, but I'm really good at collecting and presenting information, and *(Appealing to the whole group.)* I'd really like to be part of your club. If you'll have me.

JENNA. What do you think, Posy?

POSY. Me? Why me? What does everybody think?

JENNA. Spoken like a true president.

COLLETTE. Democracy at its finest.

*(***OLIVIA*** re-enters, calm, unnoticed.)*

POSY. What do you mean?

JENNA. What I mean is, Reggie's beautiful Country Cream Cupcakes tied with the savory yet delicious Bumble Bread for thirty votes, narrowly beating Janice's – I mean, Olivia's Janice's Chocolate Chip Cookies.

OLIVIA. *(Revealing herself.)* Who's Janice?

ALL. Nobody knows!

(They embrace her back into the group.)

JENNA. And while my S'mosts garnered thirty-one votes, Posy's Just Sugar Cookies received a full thirty-three!

(Cheers from all.)

POSY. I won?

COLLETTE. Despite a truly defeatist cookie name.

POSY. Oh, we can drop the word "just." That was a mistake.

JENNA. Nice work, Olivia.

OLIVIA. I didn't call it that.

(**REGGIE** *holds up the display card on which* **OLIVIA** *mistakenly wrote "Just Sugar Cookies."*)

OLIVIA. *(Genuinely aghast.)* Oh no! Did I do that? I'm so sorry, Posy!

POSY. It's okay; I could see how tense you were, trying to make everything perfect.

MEG. And it doesn't seem to have held her back; she still won.

OLIVIA. Fair and square.

JENNA. With a sugar cookie!

DUFFY. No sprinkles.

REGGIE. No icing.

JENNA. No funny shapes or fancy ingredients. You seem really nice, Posy...but HOW IS THIS POSSIBLE?

POSY. I'm not really sure. Tell me what you think.

(**POSY** *hands her a cookie. In silence,* **JENNA** *bites. Chews. Closes her eyes, takes a breath, sits down. Takes another bite and looks to the sky. It's so quiet that* **EVIE** *wakes up.*)

EVIE. *(Still groggy.)* What's going on?

REGGIE. Jenna?

(**POSY** *offers the platter up and everyone takes a cookie. They chew quietly.*)

JENNA. It reminds me of home.

REGGIE. Grandma.

MARCUS. Holidays.

COLLETTE. My best friend from kindergarten!

MEG. My brothers.

OLIVIA. Family.

EVIE. A really good hug.

BOB. Love.

JENNA. All that from this simple little cookie... Posy, making something this simple turn out this amazing is hard to do.

(A realization.)

That has to be the first lesson of Baking Club right there! Cuz I don't know about you all, but I want my baking to do that, remind people of the best parts of their lives. And, if we can do that, then...then all the rest – high school and clubs and colleges and jobs and futures – doesn't even matter!

MEG. Yeah...

OLIVIA. It still kinda matters.

MEG. Well, yeah.

POSY. Oh, wow, I can't wait to get started!

(Beat.)

But...you'll all be there, right? Olivia, no one is as organized as you. And I had no idea we had so much talent at our school. And

(With a nod to **MEG.***)* creativity, and

(With a nod to **REGGIE.***)* versatility, and

(Referencing **BOB.***)* curiosity, and

(Referencing **JENNA.***)* passion. This is... This is... We can make something really special together.

COLLETTE. While literally nourishing others.

POSY. *(To* **OLIVIA.***)* Olivia? Are you in?

OLIVIA. I'm in.

> *(The rest of the group join in with "I'm in," "Me too," etc.)*

Evie?

EVIE. I don't know. It's just...it's hard to care about things when you know they're going away.

DUFFY. Okay, but I could say the same thing about this cookie. You know, like this Sugar Cookie is not going to be around forever. You wouldn't want it to be around forever. You want it when it's at its best. And in a few years when you're thinking about that delicious sugar cookie you had when you were seventeen and you start missing the experience, the cookie will be gone, yes, but there'll be a totally different cookie in your life. Maybe it won't even be a cookie. Maybe it'll be bread with olives and pulverized chocolate, maybe it'll be a soccer game or a sunset, you know? Things that can't last even if we want them to. But whatever that future cookie is, you'll be stoked about it. Or at least, you can choose to be stoked about it. The point is, there are so many good things right here, right now. You might as well enjoy them.

> *(Bites into another cookie.)*

REGGIE. Duffy, that was like...wise.

DUFFY. *(Mouth full of cookies.)* Fank you.

> *(Bell rings. But no one is quite ready to leave.)*

EVIE. Well? Go on. Get on back to class and meet back here at lunch hour to sell the remaining stuff. I'll get here early to set up.

> *(Beat.)*

What are you all looking at? I'm going to be in the first-ever Jonesville High School Baking Club, and I'm staying awake for it!

(Cheers from all.)

DUFFY. Alright! Back to class, people!

(On the megaphone.) Back to class!

*(As they leave the auditorium...***BOB** *trails* **POSY**.*)*

BOB. You know, I did some quick math, and if we take the price of every product piece up by fifty cents, we could profit an additional fifteen percent in proceeds. And there's no question that our product quality is excellent, so...

(Exeunt. Music.)*

The End

---

*A license to produce HIGH SCHOOL BAKE-OFF does not include a performance license for any third-party or copyrighted recordings. Licensees should create their own.

APPENDIX: THE TASTERS SCENE

Productions can choose to include an optional "Tasters Scene" in which a group of student tasters performs a choreographed, stylized interpretation of tasting and reacting to the various contest entries. It can be used in place of or in conjunction with the suggested slide show between Parts One and Two.

The Tasters Scene is an opportunity to include more performers at a school or community organization, and although there is no dialogue, the scene should be treated with as much attention and rehearsal as the scripted play. I use the term "choreography" loosely; it doesn't have to look like dancing. But if your organization has dancing talent in the cast, the scene could absolutely look like a really well-rehearsed dance! If your organization has musical talent, perhaps the scene is underscored with live music. Above all, the Tasters Scene is an opportunity for creativity.

For students who are new to devising, here are some (totally optional) prompts to get you started:

1. Based on the script, what are your impressions of the students at Jonesville High?

2. Consider all the literal actions that are a part of this contest. Olivia tells us:

"Anyone who signed up to taste will come down, pay the fee to Duffy, and try everything here on display. Then they write down their vote on their ballot and drop it in the ballot box."

Consider how you might express the above actions non-literally. For example, eating a cookie is a relatively small action; what is the larger-than-life version of that action, and of the other actions that are taken in this scene?

3. Outside of The Tasters Scene, the rest of the play is pretty naturalistic. How can you contrast The Tasters Scene with the scripted scenes while staying true to the vibe of the whole play? Are there physical actions that the characters use in Part One that you can call back in a more theatrical way?

4. Since the Tasters Scene is non-literal, you can lean into the feelings around the event: Is the event joyful? Competitive? Serious? Highly anticipated? In acting terms, consider the internal actions of the Tasting Students (advocating, proving, supporting) rather than the external actions of eating and judging.

5. The Tasters Scene is perhaps a production's best chance to include music and spectacle in High School Bake-Off. So be spectacular!"